Siew-Yue Killingley was born in December 1940 in Kuala Lumpur, where, following the example of her sister, she first began writing verse as a child. She wrote some of the poems in this book in the 1960s but most them are more recent. Her publications include *The Pottery Ring: A Fairy Tale for the Young and Old* and (with Percy Lovell) *Song-pageant from Christmas to Easter, with Two Settings*. Made redundant in 1980 from her post as Senior Lecturer in English at St. Mary's College, Newcastle, the author has combined part-time university teaching with research, and has published four books on the Cantonese language.

Literature

WHERE NO POPPIES BLOW

WHERE NO POPPIES BLOW
POEMS OF WAR AND CONFLICT

Siew-Yue Killingley

Grevatt & Grevatt
Newcastle upon Tyne

Published by Grevatt & Grevatt, 9 Rectory Drive,
Newcastle upon Tyne NE3 1XT

First published 1983 on Remembrance Sunday

Design and pasteup by Grevatt & Grevatt.
Set and printed in Great Britain by Tyneside Free Press Workshop Ltd.,
5 Charlotte Square, Newcastle upon Tyne NE1 4XF.

British Library Cataloguing in Publication Data:

Killingley, Siew-Yue
Where no poppies blow.
I. Title
821'.914 PR6061.I/

ISBN 0-9507918-5-7

Price: £3.50 net plus carriage charge:
U.K.: 15% (single-copy orders) or 10% (multiple-copy orders)
Overseas: 30%. Payments from India and South-East Asia must include an extra £1.00 to cover insurance (for up to 23 copies).
33⅓% trade discount to U.K. booksellers only.

All Grevatt & Grevatt publications are non-commercially produced and priced. This book may be bought direct from the publisher or through general distributors.

For my brother and sister,
Leong Siew Wie and Khoo Siew Mun

Contents

Acknowledgments

Acknowledgments are made to the editors of the following magazines and journals, in which some of these poems first appeared: *Iron*, *Link*, *Orbis*, *Ore*, *Southeast Asian Review of English.*

Acknowledgments are made to A. D. Duncan (Parvis Books, Warkworth), Percy Lovell, and the Dean and Chapter of Durham, the respective publishers of the following booklets, in which some of these poems first appeared: *Pepper and Incense: Poems from Northumbria*, *Song-pageant from Christmas to Easter, with Two Settings*, *The Spirit of the Cathedral.*

Grateful thanks are due to many friends and colleagues, especially to Andy McGuffog and Peter Mortimer, who gave much technical advice and assistance.

Fragments: Malaya 1942?-1945

Occupation

Fragments of whispered talk
Shattered the familiar calm
Of my sweet nurse's arms
And smooth black pigtail.
Soldiers came for water, for food,
If any, and an uncle's watch.
My uncles glibly recited
The Japanese syllabary,
As they'd been instructed.
Fragments about soldiers
Touched my childish brain
In the cadence of night
Though my nurse was near:
They perform water-torture
(I guessed at its meaning),
And near the Pavilion,
A familiar cinema,
An uncle said he'd seen
Beheadings and offered
To carry me there.
My nurse screamed, pigtail
Flying, and aunts reproved—
I remained silent, reprieved.

Later, and older,
I took part in ritual.
On days of plenty
Our old cook sent me
To my dignified grandmother
To get orders for dinner.
The choice was always
Sweet potato or millet—
Which should he cook?
She calmly deliberated,
Taking her time,
And finally enunciated
'Sweet potato' or 'millet'.

The old cook received this
With an air of novelty,
And the dish of her choice
Assumed the significance
Of roast pork,
Duck,and chicken,
Things I'd heard of.

Liberation, 1945

Air attack!
What did it mean
To us as children?
Air-rending shriek
Of sirens—the signal
For shoes, woollies
And coats! The Chinese
Still believed in observing
Quaint Chinese habits
After years in the tropics.
My sister was sent off
With my brother in tow,
Hair untidy
But coats fast-buttoned,
To the rehearsed shelter
Of the banana grove.
My own coat
Of tickly maroon
At long last done up
(Wrongly buttoned up,
Then redone by my mother).
She and I
Followed in their wake,
And our servant soon after.

I had no fear but a childish wonder,
Marvelling at the noise from planes so small,
Hovering, still, above the gauzy smoke
And dropping pretty toy-like bombs
To us. I pointed, was pulled down,
And lying among the tall *lalang,*[1]
Peered up along their straight sharp edges
Pointing up to those falling toys,
Shaped like miniature black pineapples,
Gifts of either the Japanese or British.
When the air was still and the only sound
Our quiet breathing, we dashed to the grove
Of pretty banana trees hiding our neighbours
With their sweet-smelling leaves, hidden
From the sun and glowing a muted green.
We claimed my brother and sister from the crowd
And the grown-ups smiled greetings—not all
Spoke the same language. A tall Indian
Stooped, pressed a biscuit into my hand.
I looked up, confused, at my mother,
Not knowing what to do. It was pink.
She nodded permission, smiled her thanks
(And probably said something too in Malay).
I gloated at my bright pink biscuit
Glowing dimly in the palm of my hand.
I nibbled. It was musty and tasted of sacking
Soaked in oil; and till the All Clear sounded,
I stood and nibbled that tired gift
With outward enjoyment, fearing to grieve
The large Indian in the checked sarong.

1 A tall grass, *Imperata cylindrica.*

Fragments

Rhythmic chanting
Of that glib syllabary:
ka, ki, ku, ke, ko,
sa, si, su, se, so.
Hypnotic, soporific,
Mystical, poetic.
Then dinner time,
And another attack.
But this time,
While sirens shrieked
And the world splintered
Like glass, we squatted
Or sat under our large
Dinner table. My dinner
Shook in my tin plate
With a pretty red border,
And jerked out like syllables
Of grain on the floor.
Eyes reproved,
Speech being useless.
Discouraged or frightened,
I let my plate crash
Food-downwards on to concrete
With a louder percussion
Than any explosion
Of those obtrusive
Japanese-British gifts
Falling about our ears
To the poetic cadence of non-speech:
ka, ki, ku, ke, ko,
sa, si, su, se, so,
a, b, c, d, e.

Contrasts

Eyes and Teeth

(A Vietnamese Refugee)

Out of her parchment-wrapped face
Can be picked out her secret eyes,
Those dark spy-holes to suffering
Decently covered up with shutters
Of civil chat about the weather
(That sunny friend of the English),
And finally, one's life in a council flat.

Out of the human-tossing sea
She landed safe, though older
Many times over, to recover
Her lost life-line by the new sea
Of Newcastle. I caught a dark
Glimpse once of her life in death,
Quickly eclipsed by a gold-toothed smile.

Any Old Iron

In the sea-fret of Newcastle,
While the Tynerider grumbles past
(I can't bear horrid Newcastle,
Grey-damp, insularly stuck-fast),
A voice, wailing but strong,
Calls for 'any old iron', a song
Not to appeal to the overweight sage
Housewives of Gosforth (a stronghold
Of coffee-mornings), whose husbands wage
War on the cost of living, men bold
In committees but prematurely old
At home with the yawns of middle age.

I look out at 'any old iron'.
He's neither young nor old:
A mere part of the sea-fret and cold
Engendered by the coarse east-wind
Rudely biting our genteel ears
With its unwelcome kiss of cares.
His nag and cart, old rags and new,
Are trappings unfit for our suburban view;
A danger to our kids and cars;
Probably much happier behind bars...
'Yet I, who collect rags, am such as he;
Despise him, and despise me.'

Wheat and Tares

The stalls are full
And business is brisk;
The *towkay*[1] fries *kwayteow*[2]
While his boy leaps about,
Master of a rich world
Of greasy used dishes
And pliant bean-sprouts.
He fans the fickle fire,
Takes complicated orders
And shouts them out.
The *towkay* is hot,
So he airs his belly
(Like his wallet fat and shiny);
He burps nonchalantly
From the rich smell of food.

Madam Tan is out tonight
After a midnight show.
Her credible breasts bounce with quaint delight
To the tune of a few thousand dollars.
Mr. Tan nurses his pliant chest,
Sad kidneys, stomach and heart;
Madam Tan is not a weakling,
But she worries about her wart.
While the boy takes their orders,
Madam adjusts her bun
And smoothes her blouse and slacks;
Mr. Tan fears his stomach will hurt
From so much eating out:
For the rich are filled with good things
And the poor are sent empty away.

The teasing smell of *kwayteow* meets
The familiar smell from decaying heaps
Of fresh rubbish lodged in neighbouring streets
Like an irksome poor relation.
The rag-man is hard at work tonight
Separating the good rags and bad.
While the good he greedily bundles up,
The bad he callously throws away;

1 A Hokkien (Fukien) word for 'boss'.
2 A Hokkien word for a dish made of flat noodles fried in a wok.

For the good have holes to be mended,
But the bad are irredeemable.
Across the road, the fiery stall winks
Like a naughty boy at an elder.

Some Children's Faces

The road is silent now, for falling snow
Is quiet in its conquering.
Fall on my mind, in white coronation,
And freeze the grey and white
Thoughts still in a blanket of cold.
Now my silent thoughts are channelled
By the quiet snowdrift
Which crowns my mind, a cold coronation
Quietly conquering my grey heart
Still-warm through that blanket of cold.

The road for these children is silent
But for their quiet voice of starvation
Falling on the printed grey page
Of the newspaper of my mind,
Harvested from many million mute voices
Of well-trained starving children,
Unseen and unheard in public.
Now I coldly conquer my crowning compassion,
Investing my thoughts in my own dark winter,
And freeze my still heart from grief.

In Free Flight

The Prisoners

He used to lie on the Derbyshire moors
And let the cold wind blow across
His mind pictures of China, Malaya,
Cyprus, Calabria, and finally Aldabra,
Like pretty phantoms of day nightmares
On a grey screen of half-forgotten years
Spent in those places, hurrying to an awakening
To himself. He wore these coloured dreams
Like a protective cape, his last escape
If he felt even the moors too narrow
A prison for his imprisoned self
Which was always straining against fears
That he might surrender at last to sanity
And find freedom in exchanging wild hopes
For happiness such as others know it.
At such times, he gazed into the beckoning sun
And longed to exchange his safe bed
Of sweet wild moorland heather
For a hopeless pair of senseless wings.

Sometimes she remembered with tears her free
Warm youth before the cold streams
Of her illness froze her to a bed
From which she could only see
The joy and warmth of other people,
Whom she admitted with her curbed hospitality
To colour the grey screen of her mind
With the vivid activity of their days
(Since she could not herself be active).
This was her enjoyment of her share
Of narrow joy. As a child would laugh
With pure joy at the unknown ways
Of quaint animals in picture books
And the pretty doings of queens and maids,
So Margaret would complete herself
With the knowledge that she could gaze
On the pretty passage of other lives
Flitting through her flat while she trustingly
Founded her new-found freedom in their shades.

Seagull and snow

Sluggish and silent, the dazzling clouds
Of snow move towards the edges of roofs,
Sullen now that the free flight earthwards
Has ended a career as free as a bird's.
As silent as the snow, the seagull dips
And rises, no sluggard, dazzling the roofs
And the snow by its greater whiteness, like a live
Free snowflake which for a short while
Can avoid being grounded like a tired bird
And ground underfoot into melted slush.

The Seagull

Out of these hills of time
Have oozed forever the slime
Of inhuman nature glistening
Like rivers of dark grime
On a white seagull's back,
The bird which so patiently
Plunges and stretches to void
The clinging oil from its back.
Stretch back. Stetch back
And remember a time of listening
Before these hills which we climb
All unknowingly become the slime
To drown us forever. In time
Even they will darken and heave
No more to shake off the slime
Of inhuman nature, like a gull
Tired of endless plunging. In that time
There would be no time but endless
Waiting. But we are not friendless:
A human nature has descended
And nests among us. Befriended,
We brutish beings may in time
With hope become like the pure water
Which glistens in the white feathers
Of the seagull as it swoops
In free flight between the clouds
And man, gashing into the setting sun,
Like an eternal bright river
Flowing upwards in the hills of time.

Slice of Life

Relativity

When I look around me, nothing changes
But the pivotal point of my eye-ball
Which takes in at a sweep the mountain ranges
Arranged in aimlessly lonely steps, and their fall
To the plains and the sea; also the fly
Buzzing close to my eyes. All seem to glide
On the surface of an eye. And out at sea
A ship stays still on the horizon, but I descried
Through inference its real motion. Still, to me
It appears so falsely still, while what seems active
Is another trick of the eye and a change in perspective.
Then I blink my tired eye, and almost feel the image die
Out of sight as a spotted hazy truth or lie.

I looked at the world and saw a round
Eye looking back at me. On its smooth
Reflecting surface glided the mundane ground
Of its being; and it rolled gently to soothe
Itself from the granular irritation of tiny
Creatures crawling and groping on it.
They were minute and constructed like flimsy
Instruments, almost invisible against that rolling eye
Which was the seeing world. Yet they and I
Were enough to throw that solid giant into a fit
Of blinking—unless it was an optical illusion,
And our crawling movement a mere extension
Of the endless motion of the restless planet.

Then, as I look up, I see yet other greater
Worlds, all probably in continual motion.
Some are peopled, but with another
Race from ours, larger in mental proportion
To its world; whom its world sees
And recognizes as muscular pillars strong
And able to move it around, not a disease
To be wept out, and no malignant wrong
To be inferred from any mean crawling motion.

Mirrored in the large eyes of those thriving
Worlds I saw our dim reflected history of striving
Men. Then our world also looked up helplessly
At those worlds and continued to blink in calm futility.

False Exposure

This film of sand no time resists;
And eyes are clenched like futile fists
Senselessly hitting a point too distant
In the vacant view which eternally dodges
Out of focus when the strained eye
Shuts to clamp it firmly in the brain,
A dangling sandbag pounding the blurring sight.
For what is most solid in life is probably light,
Creeping between clenched lids weighed down by sand,
Heavy with the pain from a human hand
When love's life is smoothly discarded
Like some heavy afterbirth of love
Which shields from us any clear view
Of life beyond those fists clenched in dealing pain
Too ordinary to be seen or felt,
But forgotten-remembered-forgotten, as the brain
Records the fleeting shutter-action
With a click heard in camera (as you might say)
Before the naked film is exposed yet again.

Breakfast News

Now the silent gates of mercy,
Thickly closing as the North Sea mist,
Bind my eyes from painful light.
I can see no more beyond the newsprint,
Picking my way through the news and toast.
For I'm not unlike the hard-fleshed gunman,
Hard of heart in his fickle field
Of random choice of newsworthy target,
Unable to see his own bloody hand
Directed through his misty brain
By the cunning silent shutters of mercy
To hide his heart from human pain
And to hood his conscience with hell.

CONDOLENCES

Shock Absorbers

What is left to us at such times
Are our padded cells of expressions:
Deeply saddened; shocked and saddened;
Sedentarily saddened, did you say?
No, I said temporarily saddened,
That is to say, permanently shocked,
I mean, too deeply shocked to pay
Sufficient tribute to the dead,
Cushioned against further blame
In the manner of their killing.
I against my trite cushion of words
Lean backwards to peer through bars
Of woolly words without meaning,
Hoping to discover if my heart
Ever saw the plain light of grief.

A Refusal Not to Mourn

It remains a death to mourn for
Even though I'm told mourners find comfort.
Some say it's because our final death
Is not an end in creation, but rather,
A final end to that creation
In which we have our common being.
Others justify hearts' harping on the dead
By pointing to the many many years ahead
Which the departed soul could have filled
In doing this or that for himself
Or others, but now no longer years ahead
To anticipate with joy, but rather, flatness
In the daily round with living breath deflated.
Some others, like me, even recognize
That death is an end in creation, or rather,
The finite aspect or mode of life to which all
Are drawn, to rise as from a common fall.
So in death we see our common being.
But yet I mourn whenever death arises,
For human reasons too plain for reason's devices.

A Few for the Family Album

Unfinished Tapestry

How did our parents love when all their lives
Were spent in finding ways and means of ending
The fear of losing each other, and in a final binding
Of both in a mortgaged net of marriage possessions?
Since holy matrimony is an honourable estate,
An enterprise not to be lightly entered into, solemnly
We consider the cost in signing the marriage register;
For by that act we may earn a rebate
From this mundane transaction if at some later date
We too should become enmeshed in the delicate
Web which others have spun unknowingly,
Artlessly copying, though meaning to improve
On their time-warped pattern.

Did Penelope know, as she unwound her artful weaving,
The secret art of binding herself freely
To her own lost love?

A Child's Wedding

Who would have thought, who knew her
Once as a chubby toddler, that she could stir
Her lover to tenderness, awaiting her
Arrival with outward calm, the altar
Beckoning him and her to eternal oneness?

Almost like a sacrificial lamb
Clinging to its shepherd's unwilling arm,
The white figure is led ceremoniously
And takes her place next to a man
She hardly knows now except in her memory.

And then it's over. With relief
They breathe and recognize each other.
The wedding guests with kisses smother
The pair, who can only mutely stare
At each other, wonderingly. They do not dare

Believe it's true. Their joy becomes
Them: a secret fold. Two innocent lambs,
They stand hand in hand, unaware
Of friends and parents, like their first parents
Before they knew each other, or questioned

The meaning of Eden. Behind their tender thoughts,
Fenced in by the falling shadows of their night,
Lay some quickening of a hope caressed by fear
That once their parents had glimpsed a dawn
Of eternal oneness, from which they'd carelessly withdrawn.

Wedlock

While he put their car to bed,
Office thoughts wrapped around his head,
At some misty end of time
He sensed his wife's intense sublime
Absorption in her evening chores—
Baby's nappies, kids' lunch boxes,
His shirts to drip-dry (drat his snores);
'Worcesters thirty pence and Coxes
Worse at thirty-five.' Such the dusky paraphernalia
Of wedded bliss in snug suburbia,
Where expense accounts repair to bed
With female thoughts of 'there! they're fed.'

Yet sometimes as they lie in bed
As still as silent stones, he and she
Still dream they remember some foreign misty
Time before they were both born slowly
Into their present state, when quite probably
They loved, not as married couples do,
But still unfettered by the heavy catenations
Of cold routines and elaborate calculations
Such as 'is the freezer fully fed?'
But then she sighs and feigns to sleep
As his snore reminds her to repeat
A maxim that she means to keep:

That women must work and men must weep.

A New Anthem for Doomed Youth

Sing me a song of love, and I
Will try to believe it all. Sigh
No more for what loves you've lost.
Lovers soon forget the dreary frost

Of last season's finished love,
Dying a natural death by the fire
Of a new living passion. Shove
In as so much old firewood the mire

Of time-worn tangled hopes,
Once green saplings, now the gnarled ropes
Which might threaten to catch some fresh
New dear in its sinister mesh.

But as we go from love to hate
(Or worse, indifference), one day we wait
In despair for the old return of some
New feeling of love. It does not come

So we stoke up the fire carefully,
Consulting with wise men how fully
We can experiment with love to reach
Some gropingly absurd pinnacle; they teach

Us their quaint doctrine, which we follow.
But after a lifetime, there is still the hollow
Expectation of a new return to that fresh
Sapling time, before the blinding mesh

Of pointless experience had caught
Us in its stranglehold; before we were taught
The how and when of loving; when we knew
Whom we loved, and when the old held the new.

Orpheus in the Underworld

Do not look back at your drooping
Love, in the last stages of her journey
Dogging your footsteps and blankly groping
For some shaft of light to pull her firmly

Out of that bottomless cavern of night.
She was your bride and in your heart
She sang to your cosmic lyre, the might
Of its music binding her until the mortal smart

Caused by the knowing snake untimely snatched
Her out of your living embrace, bereft
You of your worshipping wife and unlatched
The gates of hell, into which the weft

And warp of your searching eternal music
Descended in a rainbow cloak of light,
Sounding out that lost love. Your forsaken sick
Soul drifted into a mourning shade, the might

Of its music lying only in a pleading dirge
So sorrowful that even the knowing suave powers
Below are moved to allow you to emerge
Alive with her again. But the deathly dower

That she brought back with her, her fear
That even after your descending into hell
For her sake you should yet forsake your dear
Love, caused you to glance back, and she fell

Again into that endless self-inflicted pit.
Remain our eternal Orpheus and descend again
And ever again with music into that silent pit
Of hell to redeem your Eurydicean world of men.

Sleep for Strength

And after love there's sleep,
Which blends the blind act
Of betrayal with the deep
Emptiness of a dream, a fact
That lovers who deny
That they betray by groan or sigh
The loss of love which they let die
Through life-long repetition
Tacitly recognize. Into sleep's damnation
Fall their love's betrayal; they lie
In sleep: in sleep is strength
To lengthen betrayed love's lily length.

Morning

In the dim cock-crow of realization
Is the echo of the lily,
Fresh in the palm of the lover
Who crushed it in dim possession.

In half-waking, cover the stark image
Of a once-living white flower
Carelessly crushed by that sleeping lover
Whose ignorance of love was to possess.

And in the final cock-crow, the dawning
Of a dim hope of new flowering
Is finally crushed in boldly denying
That love was lost through love's lying.

Mother and Man

Christmas Delivery

After the noisy upheaval, a quiet relief.
After the tedious waiting, a convinced belief
That it has been worth waiting for.
But after the build-up of joy, an unexpressed grief
That the actual moment of joy was a thief
In its elusiveness. Has it really been worth waiting for?

So after her tedious journey, what a relief
At the end of her waiting, justifying her convinced belief
That you were worth suffering for.
But after her build-up of joy, her inexpressible grief
That her kingly joy stole from her like a thief
In his elusive manhood. Yet you'd been worth waiting for.

Then after your suffering, the quiet relief
At the end of tedious waiting, and your convinced belief
That all shall have been worth waiting for.
Though your cup of joy held unspeakable grief
Which you drank for the joy of the uncomprehending, a thief
Found his elusive manhood and knew you'd been worth waiting for.

A New-style Sonnet: Manhood

Do not be afraid, in the soft
Gold-grey November, to stoop
And gently gather the fallen
Leaves of summer like a mother
Of windblown children (spent
With play, to be sweetly refreshed
By a soft kiss or caress). Never
Mind the male-masculine sneer
That in stooping so, you appear
Strangely effeminate in their eyes.

For as the yielding earth stores great beauty
In her hidden strength of creation,
So an autumnal tenderness in a man
Is a mere tint of his inner strength and glory.

My Lost Son

He went for a soldier
At a time when a mother
Could expect support from a son.
His beauty was surpassing
The beauty of women;
His love for me surpassing
His love for any woman.
His strength rippled his loving
Arm and flowed from the sun
Of his face as he bade
Me goodbye, piercing my heart
With a kiss and these words:
'Sweet mother, I'll say goodbye;
For now no mother have I.'

So he went for a soldier
And left me, his stunned mother,
To explain to all our friends
Why this child of great beauty
Surpassing all beauty
Should waste his wondrous strength
As a common soldier. No member
Of our family had done it before,
And I pray none will do it ever
Again. I'd go to the ends
Of the earth to restore
My lost son to our midst,
And his love for me surpassing
His love for any woman.

Then finally I was fetched
On a hollow grey afternoon
To his side as he hung in pain.
I sought to know him; in vain
I looked for the sun of my youth.
But he still knew his mother.
And he had a new beauty
In his suffering surpassing
The birth-pains of women
Which shone strangely as a soldier's truth.
And new strength flowed in the vein
Of his words, which he whispered
To the friend whom he loved
With a love greatly surpassing
The love of a woman:

'This woman, my love, is thy own mother;
And woman, this thy son:
For now thou hast no other.'

Thatcher's Peace

The Falklands Fracas

Wintry war with warmed-up sentiments
Unfurled by words in patriotic vein:
Our phoney war of dubious elements
To prove our mettle, for we're insane;
This game goes on in snow or rain.

Every drop of sweet man's blood
Dropped and caked in neutral mud
Clogs my brain with doubtful meaning,
Swamping thought with overweening
Postures of the great and good.

'They'll throw in the towel,
Those Argies will.
A walkover, what?
Or I'm no commander.
Not half-bad, their bombers—
What's war without losses?'
Brave boys, tip-top chaps,
Our heroes strapped to the traps
And drawn by the trappings of *Land
Of Hope and Glory*'s bland
Invitation to bury in sand
Their human thoughts in sounding grand.

And now poor peace
Pleaded vainly by Pope
And propped by people
Of dubious mettle.
The world on its axis
Is clogged with the weight
Of needless bodies
Without love, without hate.
They fill my mind's ocean
And clog up the craters
Blown in my mind
By their shattered youth's labours.

Late Autumn Poppy

Still flowering
On a lean stalk
With shielding petals
Round an arena of seed,
The very last poppy
Waits for winter's deflowering.

The Falklands' chill factor
Still-flowering in hearts
Of war-made war-mad
Valour made scatter
Of seed in wintry arena
A plausible matter.

In defence against knowledge
Of the loss of our men,
Invoke the hapless poppy
For a war-like amen.

The Parade

After the stirring songs
My voice grates with strain;
Bright colour prolongs
Me from the strain
Of seeing the hollow shades
When the picture fades.

Anthem and drum,
Boots free from scum:
The nation on wheels
To the tunes of gay reels.

We dream of the cream,
But it has gone sour;
The fountainheads stream
Love that makes me cower:
Wealth and position
Ring our damnation.

The Hero

Hero and Servant

It would be easier to recognize a brave hero
Who came in triumph, with a fanfare of trumpets,
Instead of coming as a secret thief, shamefully,
In the night. How can we be expected to know
You unless you declare yourself loudly and unequivocally
And tell us proudly that you have come as an heir
To claim your true birthright? But, you plead,
A servant does not need a herald
To say that he has come to serve.
So you will remain in the background and serve
Us patiently, but please, not in our own coin.
Since we are blind, only you can unveil our sight
With glimpses of your deep nature, surfacing as a down-and-out
Wandering the West Road when the sea-fret swarms the night;
Or as a homeless girl drowning her high hopes in the Underground;
And sometimes, even at Christmas, as an unwanted baby
Drowning its sweet life in our human sea of limiting love.
Since we are deaf, only you can help us turn again and listen
To your loving song of peace and mundane death
And to sympathetically vibrate our heartstrings to your pure notes
Sounding through the drowning din of our world's demands.
For often we grow deaf to the constant sweetness
Of a familiar daily voice, forgetfully switching off
What we daily expect to hear, though its death
Would entomb us in its sudden echoing silence.
In a battle for survival, we grow blandly blind to the true nature
Of the soldier fighting nearest to us. For at Emmaus
The two could not see, through blind proximity,
The heroism of the third until his unlooked for revelation
Of himself in that simple act of service at table.

The Human Race

In memory of Dermot MacDowell Killingley (1900-1980), cavalry officer, later ordained priest

He rides to stand still,
His wheaten body, straining on a frame,
To airy thinness beat, though earthy
Still.

He rides in a stupor of prayer,
While his stretched wooden steed, instead
Of bearing up his earthly strength,
Instils

Man's defeat. But then, his wheaten body,
Sown unlike the other two, unnaturally,
Strengthens the wooden frame while whitening
Still,

And his unearthly eye is cast
On his flagging outriders, the earthly
Two, one at least hell bent on losing
Still.

The other is spurred on by a look
And voice which lash into his wooden frame,
And quickened spirit hopes to gain his mastery
Still.

And so we ride, not in a stupor of sleep,
But in waking knowledge of the sown field
Where the central moving figure, mastering his race,
Makes what outriders' speed we muster stand
Still.

Remembrance Sunday

I am too young and unscathed to fully remember
The grim meaning of Remembrance Sunday.
But for many this pretty poppy will never
Be a mere symbol of a happy summer's day.

For many have suffered who now sharpen their memory
On the black whetstone of past hate and fear
Stocked in their lifetime with the armoury
Of war, to be trotted out for inspection each year.

Still, I am not too young to sometimes remember
The meaning of love's daily trial and dying.
And this red emblem worn so bravely forever
Recalls for me the death of mankind, lying

For centuries on our hands, a red reminder
Of the blood we spill daily from a true nature
Flush in the wine but drained in the blanched wafer
Donated to us to help us bravely remember

To emulate the warrior whose soul fought his body,
Cringing in human fear from the enveloping sea
Of pain as he offered up his own blood and body,
Saying, 'do this in remembrance of me.'

Holy Week 1982

For Percy Lovell

I Prelude and Prophecy: Monday 5th April

Holy Saviour or mad drunkard
Reeling in a wine-sprinkled dance?
He will tread and stamp
With crude variations
The stately measure
Of a royal dance.

I do not reject this outpouring
Of her infamous love, dipping
Into her inexhaustible jar—
Let this remain on my head,
This rash action; do not mar
Her act, smoothing my path to the dead.
You who question her dipping
As true charity will slip
From truth as you dip
With me in the dish.
And one will even wish
He'd never been born
After dipping into false coin
To lubricate his lying tongue
To know me as master with a kiss.

II The Inclination: Tuesday 6th April

My ear inclined towards truth;
Therefore I fell among torturers.
An ear that inclined to falsehood
Was felled and restored by the hand
Of the man bent on suffering,
Whose ear heard the fear of the dark.
Cold morning's call of justice
Fell on the stone dead ears
Of the false, asserting
A preference for their own murderer,
Not a falsely-crowned king.
One dipped his bland fingers in water
As coolly as the other at supper,
When his reasoning fell on stone deaf ears,
Grating against them like sprinkling sand
To mark out a guilty tattoo.
So the ear of the man inclined
To right the error fell prey
To other reasons, and gave way
To the erection of your cross.
And from the stretching of that hour
You rose erect in manhood's flower,
Stooping only to incline your ear
To our false testimony of love.

III Passover: Wednesday 7th April

Judas inclined his ear to his heart
And dipped his hand in silver.
At night he kissed for his lover's blood
And passed from day forever.

'No, I never will deny my Lord'
(My hand on heart or silver).
My ear, attuned to heart's own voices,
Recalled at cock-crow to shatter.

I hear the pump of fear in my heart.
It will beat to the sound of silver
Unless you revoke that will and recall
Your lamb at your own Passover.

IV Maundy Thursday: 8th April

Pilate prevaricated, deliberated;
Herod delightedly contributed
Some mockery in his own coin.
And a friendship was freshly minted.

Judas' silver in mint condition
Scattered, sprinkling the Potters' Field.
The Jews tendered their false petition
To Pilate—their murderer to yield.

I am struck in the dubious metal
That bought my master to Calvary
To buy me at the last battle
With coin not minted as money.

V Good Friday: 9th April

The Wicklow hills in summer weather
Are dipped in purple, with a golden haze.
There among the gorse and heather,
Peaceful lovers can lie and laze.

There among the thorny gold
Of speckled gorse and purple heather,
My love for love of silver sold
Was crowned, and burnt by thongs of leather.

Behold the man, a thorny crown
Of gorse and robe of royal heather.
My love from suffering's height glanced down
To breathe at last, 'behold, thy mother.'

They despoiled my joy in the summer gold
And gorgeous dye of purple heather,
When my love for love of men was sold
And paid in mingled blood and water.

VI The Stone: Easter Even, 10th April

No silver was paid
For the box of sweets
In which my Lord was laid.

The stone jar of ointment
Was a box of sweets
For my Lord's interment.

Alabaster for silver
As pure act of charity
Could've served him better.

But more poor for silver
Can always be bought;
My love lost forever
In a poor bargain was caught.

From my body, now stone,
They stole him, my own.
They stole him, disowned him,
He remained still as a stone.

My body was chaste
In which my sweet was encased;
Also virgin the stone
Where he lies all alone.

This white stone is all
That is left to recall
My box of sweets, stolen
By men to be broken.

VII Easter Day: 11th April

Early at cock-crow
When both grey and white
Are the same shadow,
I paled at the spite
Of those who could steal
And hide the body
Of my Lord.

A hole in the dawn
Of the grey cock-crow
Denying he was borne
To rest in the shadow
Of that box. Who could steal
And hide the body
Of my Lord?

Inside the paling stone
Box, a lightning white
Figure, like stone:
'No fear, no spite;
For no one can steal
The risen body
Of our Lord.'

VIII Postscript: The Workman

Your hand was the hammer · that hammered and hit
The hearts of frail humans · we fashioned the hate.
Your path marked with palms · you pursued into Jerusalem;
Anointed at Passover · prepared for your passing.
Pilate was imprisoned · by his own person;
Poured water on palm · and pushed him in prison.
Herod in hilarity · hurled my hero heavenwards.
He harrowed our hell · with a crown unlike Herod's,
So that my marriage to money · was marred by his martyrdom;
No kissing or lying · in the new king's kingdom.
By my lies you have laid · a living causeway
From this world to the next · to welcome the stray,
Enabling the wayward · to anchor their wandering.
Hammer hard now new hearts · hallowed by your harrowing.

Songs for War and Peace

Song of Praise

Praise to the poor in spirit · poorly proportioned in earth;
In heaven's high halls · handsomely rewarded.
Sing to the sorrowing · a new song of sweet sorrow.
Among mankind the meek · mankind will make;
Food to the fervent · fighting for my faith's sake.
Unless you mete mercy · how shall mercy be meted
To you and your young · and the yokĕd in age?
Let hearts clear as crystal · mirror their king's image
To show his lost sheep · the shepherd's strong shoulder
To carry them carefully · and their cares lighten.
Make peace among peoples · as true pupils of peace;
And inherit heaven's riches · by adhering to his behest:
By losing lightly of heart · be merrily led to your maker.

Psalm 23

Like the homely shepherd of new-born lambs
In the spring on Muggleswick Common (too weak
To stand on their own spindly legs
And trembling against the east wind's bleak,
Some bleating for their warm lost sheep),
You have mercifully provided for us, snugging
Us firmly against your rocky shoulder
And feeding us coaxingly from your own loving hand,
Strong with the strength of the hidden meek
Grass which gently opens up a barren boulder.

And sometimes, when we've aimlessly run
Ourselves out of breath, foaming and dashing
Like some mad sheepdog dashing in flight
From its own cruel tearing pains;
Or like the mortally infected human being
Racing madly from himself, to shun
The fearful sight of water; you stretch
Out your rippling green meadow arms

To take us to your fertile breast
To feed, while you suck out all fear of infection.

Often we discover too late we are breaking
Our brittle souls against a soft wall
Of sand, deceived by its gentle cunning
Give when we lean heavily against its pall-
Like form; for there's precious little to fill
Our parched minds with these days (as all
Who've lived in the dead past have always said).
But again you take us gently by the hand
And brand us suddenly with your own name in red
To show us the rocky road to peace.

Once, in a mad emptiness of sorrow,
When the disappearing dead the drear dread
Of my own death uncovered, and fear
Dashed me down as I scampered to you,
Your shepherd's staff sang a strange stave
Of chords, its final augmented triad of hope
A sweet cadence too discordant a song for the baying
Wolves' ears to endure; and my fear
Of death and bereavement dissolved in its notes
Like the gradual evaporation of a tear.

Not many of us can be rich kings
In this world, or else your poor camel
Would slide through that narrow needle's eye
As smoothly as the easy escape of a sigh
When we know that a cruel trial is over.
But the spilling food and drink at your altar
So freely and readily given (though never
As readily received) anoint and become
My own flesh and spirit, to ward off forever
Despair, as I keep counting the cost on earth.

As you have poured sweet mercy, mild Lord,
On one who deserves none or little,
Show me how to show mercy if called on
So to do, much as I'd rather distil
My anger, and feed on its pure cold crystal,
The stronger to grow and to destroy him who lords
It over me, enjoying the fruits of his evil.
For your rough shed was my new-born shelter;
And at last I'll have no other, though bleakly I might shudder
Like the bereft lambs in the spring on Muggleswick Common.

Singing Practice

For Christine Ring

Of all beings who have been given voice
To sing and praise their creation, man's voice
Is surely the sweetest and the very worst.
Much as I love to lie and listen
To the musical approach of day in a burst
Of birdsong, I'd think myself in prison
If I heard no voice but a bird's, sweet
Though it may be, and its untaught song
A repeated note of joy for me to greet
Each new-sung day. But how long
Will the sweetness of human voices last?
Can a flute's mellow voice withstand a bugle's blast?
The birds practise their peaceful song
As a happy fact of nature, instinctively.
They do not sing of evil or of wrong
Towards each other. We practise bitterly
In skilfully singing our songs of war,
To orchestrate our hate against your operatic design
Of peace, stirring our audience with religious awe—
That they must fight and kill, or else resign
All manhood. Teach our souls to sing
A new song, not devoid of sorrow,
But one that might one morning wring
Our hearts with pity—so that we needn't borrow
The voice of a bird to praise the dayspring
From on high. Tune our voices; let them wing
Home to you like the bird attuned to its nest.
And let our final silence be no more than a bar's rest.

Drought: By the Waters of Babylon

By the dry rivers of our own wringing
We sit down, too stunned to weep.
The memory of their abandoned musical flowing
Makes us keep time silently, longing for some kind sleep
To take us back in time, to bask again
In their rainbow spray, and to hear once more
Their liquid melody, once the life of men
Who are now cast up dead on an unearthly shore.
For now, as if to emulate that hollow dryness,
Our throats gape open in futile dumbness;
And the song which would have rolled out
Is buried forever in a parched silence; the shout
Of joy that should have signalled freedom
Commuted into the heavy breathing of Adam
When he became the gasping prisoner of a snake.
In the coils of a strange grasping land
How can we sing while we are falsely awake?
We have exchanged a rock, your source, for sand
As our foundation, one that could insidiously destroy
(Though in a sandpit it's a child's innocent toy)
Our last memory of the early streams
Of mercy by sucking us, gasping, into its calm surface.
Even Lady Macbeth, in her wildest dreams
Of mad ambition to torture herself childless,
Would suffer less torment than the endless hell
We would be in were we once to forget
The last glimpse of those full rivers which tell
Us by their present drought whose blood we let.

Song of the Blind

Out of the depths of my earthly despair
I sang a new song: why have I
Been blindly forsaken and left to cry
Alone, my life drawn by the world's shadowy snare?

Out of the depths of the unearthly despair
Of my mother's womb I sang in fear.
You drew me out, blinded, and held me near
To you,my life now shaded in your drawing care.

Out of the depths of all the dark
Pits of death which my life has known
You have sung me a new song, grown
From the mystery of your life, like a sombre lark.

Now out of the depths of the dark earth
Of my making, let me sing a new song
To the live accompaniment of your coming, long
Shadowed from me by the blindness drawn from my birth.

Contrapuntal Plainsong: My Love Is a Lily[1]

I looked for my love among the cold thorns
Of roses, and found him a lily among thorns.

I looked for my love in the wild forest
And found him an apple tree among the rest.

I looked for my love among the world of men
And found him a son lost and found again.

I looked among wild revellers for my love
And he protected me with his large banner, love.

I look for quiet peace under that banner,
And find shrouded there a child called by love
To sweeten with fruit our knowledge, once bitter,
By piercing his live lily on the cold thorns of our love.

1 The subject of each line in the quatrain is set against (and is a mirror-image of) each of the subjects shown in the four couplets, which partly explains the title.

Nuclear Vision

Grass-scape

At my birth
I was pushed
And rushed on to the lush
Grassy days of man
Flourishing greenly
In a deflowering field.

And at my death
I was blown
By an expiring breath
Flattening those days
To a cold foreshortened
Golden autumn field.

Lullaby

When the sleeping hand of man
Raises up an ancient dream
Hovering on the banks of sleep
And shifts the sand-storms from the deep,
Then the sleeping guns of war
Thunder on the dreaming shore
Pressed down by the shoring hands
Helpless to prevent the bands
Raised in futile infant dreams:
Brave new world sunk now in streams
Of tears which blind the opening eye,
Mirrors of fresh ways to die.

And There Shall Be No Weeping

On that endless day of wrath we'll sit
Among the fragments of our hearts.
Who can sing in praise of sorrow,
Choked by their broken vocal chords
Hanging on the memory of vanished trees?
That day shall play out a lasting song
Upon a shattered harp in silent Babylon,
Impotently telling of our once-humanity.

In the captive silence of that day
Shall sit our shattered hearts,
Not pulsing with the song of blood,
With lost and broken human chains
Too heavy to draw out a mourning song
Or the forgotten memory of tears.
That day shall peal out the last life-toll,
And choke on the dry fact of that telling.

Desolation in the Vein

When daylight breaks on skin and bone,
When water shrivels up the stone,
The sun in darkness hides its colours
In shame and pride of blackened flowers;
The army of the dead arises,
And baring skin as flags, enquires
Which camp is ready now for flight.

As darkness breaks on man alone,
His mettle hardens into stone.
Its molten fire hides its manly colours
In shame that fear has blackened powers
The army of the dead has seized.
No camp resists death's flowers released,
And flies death's flag with grin and bone.

CND March[1]

In Flanders fields the poppies blew;
We march in memory, two by two,
And mark our place. In time the sky
Will shroud no birds; no vultures fly
Above the quaintly dead below,
Rosy in man-made sunset glow,
All love reduced to fiction's lie,
More cunningly complete than Flanders fields.

In Flanders fields, if we had died,
The living poppies would prove we'd tried
To mark our place as men of peace.
But in the future, life's release
Will not be marked by grave or flower.
And silent minutes will have no power
To sound the last post for peace,
More hollow than the lie of Flanders fields.

Two Armies

Across the paling curve of sunset
They aim in pointed wedge-formation.
One or two in shivering blunder
Cause its victory shape to quiver,
But on the whole, they fly in peaceful
Purpose, knowing their aim, relentless.

Beyond the pale of emptied sunset
They aim their pointed whole destruction.
Beyond all knowledge of human blunder
They snatch from doubtful victory's quiver,
And as one whole, emit in blissful
Power, forgetting their aim, relentless.

1 This poem is an antithesis to John McCrae's 'In Flanders fields the poppies blow', which sees meaning in the First World War dead only in terms of others taking up 'our quarrel with the foe'. The last line in each stanza imitates in rhythm the way in which well-drilled soldiers on the parade ground change step on the march, one of the many cunningly executed displays which compel our admiration. Each last line has the same irregular rhythm (x / x x x / x / x /), in contrast to the overall regular rhythm in the other lines.

End of British Summer Time

(Written on 1st November 1981 for Remembrance Sunday)

Push back the clock
To reset the new time.
Forget all summer madness
In new winter's mean time.
From ten minutes to midnight
We settled once on four:
Four minutes to midnight
At cold midwinter's door.
From taut minutes to midnight
We sprang and touched on nought:
Nought minutes to nothing's gate
Annihilate love and hate.
Press on the catch spring
To release the new season
Of hope in flawed spring,
Cold and dead to reason
As the hand moves to ring
The last midnight all shattering,
My last, our last second,
To damn all nature's spring.

Recall the Last Trumpet

In a white darkness of dawn,
A bland sun bathes the wounds
Of a star shattered world.
And an erstwhile Sunday red
With the sunny poppy of the dead
Of two world wars is blacked out
Of experience. Not one dismembered
Member of dishonoured mankind
Is buttonholed to trumpet the bland
Blasphemy of man's sleight of hand
In remembering the fast dead members
Of a past living world of wars.
Achieve the impossible,
And remember the future
(A new Hiroshima)
Where no poppies blow.

Envoy

I will sing unto the Lord as long as I live:
I will praise my God while I have my being.

PSALM 104

Also published by Grevatt & Grevatt

The Only True God: Works on Religion by Rammohun Roy, selected and translated from Bengali and Sanskrit by D. H. Killingley.
ISBN 0 9507918 1 4. £3.20 net plus carriage: £3.60 (U.K.); £4.60 (overseas).

John Henry Newman: A Man for Our Time? Edited by T.R. Wright.
Contributors: T. R. Wright, Michael Ramsey, Ian Gregor, P. J. FitzPatrick, J. D. Holmes, Bernard Reardon.
ISBN 0 9507918 4 9. £3.95 net plus carriage: £4.54 (U.K.); £5.15 (overseas).